BIG IDEAS for YOUNG THINKERS

JAMIA WILSON ○ ANDREA PIPPINS

WIDE EYED EDITIONS

CONTENTS

TRUTH

CULTURE

CREATIVITY

HAVE YOU EVER BEEN TOLD THAT YOU ASK TOO MANY QUESTIONS?

I HAVE. MY NAME IS JAMIA, AND GROWING UP, I LOVED NOTHING MORE THAN DEBATING THEORIES ABOUT THE WORLD. As the child of two professors who hungrily read the newspaper each day, I begged my mother to speed up her ritual of sipping a steamy cup of lemon tea while reading the news, so I could review the headlines and then check out the comics.

I always wanted to know about the root causes of things, beyond what I could ask a teacher or my parents throughout the day. I delighted in getting to the heart of a matter and then finding another rabbit hole to swoosh down into a new portal of information and imagination. Looking back, I realize that the most helpful information I received came in the form of books.

Reading other people's ideas inspired me to write down my own thoughts and gave me the ability to think critically, to challenge myself, and sometimes, to change my mind when a seed of wisdom bloomed into a garden of new ideas.

DO YOU FEEL THE FIRE OF CURIOSITY ABOUT THE "HOWS" AND THE "WHYS" OF THE WORLD? IF SO, KEEP READING.

Eventually, my parents started giving me additional "homework" after my schoolwork was done. After I asked why most of the big thinkers in my school books were mostly white men from Europe, they asked me to write book reports and organize presentations at home about diverse writers, poets, philosophers, scientists, theorists, and visionaries from around the world.

> **The questions are often more important than the answers.**

This question about why we didn't learn about more thinkers from communities as diverse as ours preoccupied me, and as an adult it led me to work as the executive director and publisher for the Feminist Press, an educational nonprofit organization founded to amplify diverse, feminist perspectives.

We make sense of the world around us based on thoughts and beliefs that we hear in our homes, schools, the media, museums, and—for some of us—in places of worship. But it's up to us to develop our own theories about the world rather than simply absorbing what we're told. We need to consider all sorts of facts and ideas, and connect the dots in a way that makes sense for us.

One way we can practice being thinkers and truth-seekers is by reading about, talking about, and sharing ideas. This is called "philosophy." The word philosophy means "love of wisdom," and anyone who wonders about big questions on life and the universe is a philosopher. By choosing this book, you have shown that you are a philosopher, too! Even if you don't look or sound like the people who are usually upheld as the best and brightest geniuses in your textbooks, in the library, or on TV, your questions and thoughts are just as meaningful.

In this book, you'll discover that the questions are often more important than the answers. And you'll develop your skills in considering a variety of ways of looking at an issue to decide where you stand. Maybe you'll even come up with your own big idea or new question. If so, congratulations! Your inquiring mind is what is needed to help create a better world.

Look up names in **bold** on the timeline (pages 60), or words that are underlined in the glossary (page 62) to help with understanding.

So welcome to this book, and the adventure of the mind that we'll take together.

THE BIG IDEAS GUARANTEE:
What happens when we disagree?

AS WE BEGIN OUR JOURNEY TOGETHER, WE MUST BE CLEAR ON THE "BIG IDEAS GUARANTEE"—THAT WE ALL HAVE QUESTIONS, BUT WE WON'T ALWAYS HAVE THE SAME ANSWERS.

Ideas are powerful and informative, whether we absorb them, challenge them, or let them go. As a writer, speaker, and <u>activist</u>, I've spent a lot of time exploring important issues, both with people who share my viewpoints and with those who strongly disagree.

Although most humans value peace, freedom, safety, good health, partnership, education, and protecting the planet, we often have different approaches and solutions for how to achieve these goals. While there is always much to debate, we can often find common ground through shared experiences and points of connection.

It can be frustrating when we don't see eye to eye with people in our community, especially our loved ones, but talking openly and respectfully about differences of opinion can help us learn a lot about ourselves and others. Practice these tried-and-true tactics for engaging in debates and courageous discussions:

• Show up and be present. Don't dismiss a discussion just because you disagree with what someone is saying.

> **We all have questions, but we won't always have the same answers.**

6

• Listen deeply without interrupting. Be prepared to learn that you might be wrong about something, and don't assume the worst of the person you are talking to.

• Mind your body language. Your non-verbal communication tells a story, too.

• Look for common ground and areas of agreement, and acknowledge them with a spirit of goodwill.

• Remember that courage is contagious—when you explore an issue with an open mind, it inspires others' willingness to grow, too.

• Acknowledge to yourself that we all have <u>biases</u>. Try to release your own, and then listen deeply.

• Respect insights from people who have been affected or impacted by an issue directly, or have lived experience of a topic.

• Don't talk down to people. Be humble and assume they are just as smart and worthy of being heard as you are.

• Take responsibility. We all make mistakes and sometimes the impact of our words doesn't reflect our good intentions. Be ready to honestly acknowledge if you have caused offence—remember that it won't be the first or last time a human has done this.

• Be curious and ask open-ended questions without an agenda. If you find yourself having a knee-jerk reaction, take a deep breath and ask a question to learn more.

• Be confident about your ideas, but remain humble. Remember: "No one knows everything, together we know a lot." (Anti-opression Resource Training Alliance)

• Set healthy boundaries. If a conversation turns into bullying, name-calling, or otherwise becomes unsafe or unhealthy, end it. Get support and seek connection from a trusted adult, friend, or ally.

You can add to this list of tactics as you build up experience in discussing big ideas. What have you learned that helps you during disagreements?

IDENTITY

WHO AM I?

HOW DO I KNOW I EXIST?

WHAT IS AN INDIVIDUAL?

IS RACE REAL?

WHAT IS GENDER?

WHO AM I?

HAVE YOU EVER HAD A FAVORITE SUPERHERO FROM A COMIC BOOK OR MOVIE? If so, you probably know their origin story—in other words, how they came to be in their imaginary world. You may even be inspired by this tale of how they learned to own their strengths in order to improve the world.

You have your own real-life origin story, which you were born into. Depending on your family's scientific, religious, cultural, philosophical, or political beliefs, you might have heard different ideas and stories about why humans are here on Earth and how we know we are real.

So, what exactly makes a person who they are? For thousands of years, thinkers, poets, artists, scientists, politicians, and visionaries across the globe have explored this question. A form of the phrase "know thyself" is said to have origins in ancient Egypt, and was later carved into the Temple of Apollo at Delphi in ancient Greece, which shows how important this question has been to people for a long time.

> **Wisdom comes from questioning, not thinking that you already have the answers.**

The ancient Greek philosopher **Socrates** (Sok-*ruh*-teez) taught his students that "the unexamined life is not worth living." He taught that only by working to understand ourselves do our lives have any meaning or value. This was a lesson about self-awareness that has influenced human understanding to this day.

Although Socrates was known as "the wisest man in Greece," he argued that he knew nothing at all! That's because he believed that wisdom comes from questioning, not from thinking that you already have the answers. He encouraged his students to debate ideas so they could learn how difficult it is to provide definite answers (or absolute truths) to philosophical questions.

Many thinkers have wondered if humans' search for deeper meaning is what makes us unique among animals. They have pondered if—and how—our bodies and minds work together to help us understand ourselves and our existence.

These thinkers have shared some viewpoints, and been in conflict over others. They have explored different approaches and given different reasons for why we have imaginations, reflect on memories, create and discover new things, and manage our behavior in certain ways. But they are all united in their curiosity, and their interest in why humans are curious—just like you are reading this book in order to learn more.

Look at the quotes by key thinkers on the opposite page. What do they mean to you?

551 BCE – 479 BCE

CONFUCIUS

Chinese philosopher

"What you know, you know; what you don't know, you don't know. This is true wisdom."

428 BCE – 348 BCE

PLATO

ancient Greek philosopher

"Thinking—the talking of the soul with itself."

384 BCE – 322 BCE

ARISTOTLE

ancient Greek philosopher

"All men by nature desire to know."

1058 – 1111

IMAM AL-GHAZALI

Persian Islamist philosopher

"Knowledge exists potentially in the human soul like the seed in the soil; by learning the potential becomes actual."

1632 – 1677

BARUCH SPINOZA

Dutch philosopher

"We feel and know that we are eternal."

1948 –

PATRICIA HILL COLLINS

American feminist author and scholar

"The power of a free mind consists of trusting your own mind to ask the questions that need to be asked."

1974 –

ROXANE GAY

American feminist author and scholar

"What I know and what I feel are two very different things."

Hypatia
(AD370-415)

Roman mathematician

"Reserve your right to think, for even to think wrongly is better than not to think at all."

Siddharta Gautama (Buddha)
(563-483BCE)

Nepalese spiritual leader

"The mind is everything. What you think you become."

Bishop George Berkeley
(1685-1753)

Irish philosopher

"To be is to be perceived."

bell hooks
(1952-)

American feminist, author, and scholar

"Knowledge rooted in experience shapes what we value and as a consequence how we know what we know as well as how we use what we know."

Ludwig Wittgenstein
(1889-1951)

Austrian philosopher

"The limits of my language means the limits of my world."

Dan Siegel
(1957-)

American psychiatrist

"The mind is not just brain activity."

HOW DO I KNOW I EXIST?

FOR CENTURIES, PHILOSOPHERS HAVE EXPLORED THE QUESTION OF WHAT OUR "SELF" ACTUALLY IS, AND HOW WE KNOW IT EXISTS. Is this "self" defined by our mind, body, or spirit, or a combination of these? Is the mind part of the body, or does the mind imagine the body?

As early as AD 1002, **Ibn Sina**, an Arabic physician, asked "Do I exist?" and began exploring how we notice the feelings we have in our bodies and in our minds. Ibn Sina was known as one of the most influential scientist-philosophers of his time. He studied cause and effect and searched for logical proof of the existence of God. He wrote a thought experiment called the "floating man" to explain his beliefs about our existence. He argued that, if a person was magicked into existence but floating in the air with a blindfold on so that they didn't have any physical sensations, they would still know they existed. Therefore, we can have self-awareness of our existence without any input from our senses. For Ibn Sina, the "self" that the floating person is aware of, is the soul.

Hundreds of years later, French philosopher **René Descartes** came to a similar idea. He thought a lot about how we know that we really exist, and believed that our body's senses (sight, smell, and so on) could not always be relied upon to show us the truth. However, he believed that the fact that our minds think, sense, and believe proves that we are real. If we didn't exist, we wouldn't be thinking in the first place. As he wrote: "I think; therefore I am."

Descartes believed that these thinking and reasoning abilities are the key essence of what it is to be human (read more about human nature on pages 26–27). He also argued that human beings are born with certain in-built ideas, such as knowledge of God.

British philosopher **John Locke** thought quite differently. He taught that we are born knowing nothing at all, like blank sheets of paper. He said that we only learn through using our five senses to experience the world; and that our mind then examines and combines the information in lots of different ways (read more about knowledge on pages 48–49). **David Hume** built on Locke's ideas, and argued that we absorb information through our senses and feelings, and use this to build our understanding of the world.

We've seen here how thinkers in the past have come at the same question from different perspectives. Are our bodies in charge, our thoughts like computer programs running in the hardware of our brains and being affected by what our physical bodies touch or hear? Or do our thoughts and feelings determine our physical experience, imagining a physical reality which doesn't even exist?

Whatever ideas immediately resonate with you, it's crucial to think about a variety of ideas while constructing and considering your unique take on the subject.

WHAT IS AN

HAVE YOU EVER CONSIDERED WHAT MAKES YOU UNIQUELY "YOU"? Although we all share the fact that we're flesh and bone, humans are diverse beings who often look, feel, think, and behave differently.

On pages 12–13, we looked at how complex it can be to define our "self" in terms of a body, mind, and spirit. So what separates us from others and makes each of us an individual? Do we actually have a single "self" throughout our life, or even beyond death?

For thinkers such as **Epicurus**, the mind is a function of the brain as an organ (body part), and it stops when our bodies pass away. For spiritual philosophers such as **Siddhartha Gautama**, our sense of self can expand and transform like our bodies do with time and age. I like to think of how shapeshifters in mythology and folklore can willfully change their form and identity when imagining this idea.

Each individual human shares the Earth with billions of other individuals, and this has led many thinkers to ponder how we ought to get on with each other. In different cultures and at different times, people have placed more importance on "the individual" as an idea. "Individualism" is loosely the idea that the rights and freedoms of the individual are the most important things in any society. British philosopher **John Stuart Mill** was one of the idea's most passionate defenders. He said in 1859 that people should be free to do whatever they wish,

> **Humans are diverse beings who often look, feel, think and behave differently.**

"I will not let ANYONE walk through my mind with their dirty feet."

INDIVIDUAL

?

as long as they don't harm other people.

However, writing about the U.S.A. at a similar time, the French political philosopher **Alexis de Tocqueville** wrote that the individualism of American society caused people to be *only* concerned with the well-being of their own family and friends.

Communication can be a challenge when finding common ground with other individuals. John Locke thought that we assume other people think the way we do, based on what we see in their behavior. He said that although we can pick up cues from other people based on their speech, tone, body language, and movements, we can't truly understand what's in their mind without them communicating it to us using language.

Of course, we may still interpret their meaning

wrongly. The way we view the world and communicate our emotions, both verbally and non-verbally, might be very different than the way another individual does. Each one of us has our own genetic footprint, cultural background, and personal context, and this variation leads us to understand and experience situations and relationships in many different ways.

The differences between us are wonderful, but sometimes it can feel difficult for us to celebrate our own individuality. As **e.e. cummings** said, "To be nobody-but-yourself—in a world which is doing its best, night and day, to make you everybody else—means to fight the hardest battle which any human being can fight; and never stop fighting." Or as **Gandhi** put it…

MOHANDAS (MAHATMA) GANDHI

(1869-1948)

Indian activist

IS

"R-A-C-E." IT'S A WORD PEOPLE ARE OFTEN SCARED TO TALK ABOUT. BUT WE NEED TO TALK ABOUT IT, IN ORDER TO DEBUNK MYTHS AND STOP INJUSTICE.

On page 10, we talked about origin stories for superheroes and our individual "selves". But did you know that every single human is connected to the same shared origin story?

As *Homo sapiens*, which is the human species we all belong to, we're all related to each other. That's right—you share lineage with every other human on the planet, no matter the differences in your eye color, height, skin, hair color, or hair texture.

Modern-day humans originated from the earliest human ancestors, who evolved over millions of years from another group of primates in East Africa. Our species, *Homo sapiens*, appeared around 200,000 years ago. While most of human evolution happened in Africa, some of our earliest relatives moved out of Africa to Asia, and later to the continents we know as Europe and Australia.

As the earliest members of our human family began to adapt to new climates and environments over time, we became more varied in our outward appearance due to shifts in our surroundings. For example,

humans who lived closer to the equator tended to have deeper skin tones, to increase their skin's protection from the sun's bright rays. People living in colder climates had lighter skin.

As our ancestors migrated over time—sometimes willingly, sometimes tragically due to force and violence from slavery or colonialism— human diversity became more commonplace in regions far from our relatives' origins. While it's true that on the surface you can see clear differences between how some groups of people look, race is not biological, scientific, or real.

Race is an illusion that humans have historically— and presently—turned into reality, in order to identify people who appear to share similar ancestry or to promote stereotypes or systems that benefit one group over another. It has a real impact in our society because, throughout human history, race has been used as a social marker to isolate, control, or abuse people who look different from the dominant group in power.

Although it's wrong to judge, mistreat, harm, or be biased against other humans based on their perceived racial identity, ignoring the impact hundreds of years of social inequality has caused expands the problem instead of addressing it.

RACE

REAL

While race itself may not be "real" in a scientific sense, racism remains a global problem. Racism is the mindset that emerged from European scientists in the 17th century onward to justify colonialism, slavery, and harming and displacing <u>Indigenous</u> peoples worldwide. Racism can only be countered by addressing it, not by pretending it doesn't exist. That's why it's important to understand history, pay attention, and stop myths and <u>discrimination</u> by speaking up.

Here are some big ideas about race from thinkers around the world:

KAILIN GOW
(UNKNOWN-)
Asian American author

"Do not diminish who you are. Your gender, your heritage, your identity. That's what makes you unique."

FRANTZ FANON
(1925-1961)
French West Indian psychiatrist and philosopher

"I want the world to recognize with me the open door of every consciousness."

CHIMAMANDA NGOZI ADICHIE
(1977-)
Nigerian feminist author

"Race doesn't really exist for [white folks] because it has never been a barrier. Black folks don't have that choice."

JAMES BALDWIN
(1924-1987)
American writer and activist

"Color is not a human or a personal reality. It is a political reality."

ROBIN DiANGELO
(1956-)
American writer and scholar

"No cross-racial relationship is free from the dynamics of racism in this society."

WHAT IS GENDER?

FROM THE MOMENT BABIES ARE BORN, THEY RECEIVE MESSAGES ABOUT WHO THEY ARE AND WHO THEY WILL GROW UP TO BE. Although times are changing, kids often receive signals about how they should look, act, dress, speak, and play. For example, girls and boys are often given different colored clothes and toys, and may be rewarded for behavior that matches stereotypes about gender in society.

> **"Stereotyping of females begins when the doctor says, 'It's a girl.'"**

Stereotypes happen when people are pigeonholed into an unjust idea that all people who share their background or traits are the same. These oversimplified ideas of who and how people are limit our true understanding of others and ourselves. Have you ever heard phrases like "Boys will be boys" or "All girls like pink?" Those are stereotypes. Boys are frequently told not to cry, and "be brave." Girls are often told to smile, and not to be "too bossy." As **Shirley Chisholm** said in the 1970s, "Stereotyping of females begins when the doctor says, 'It's a girl.'"

Gender is a broad spectrum, like a rainbow, that includes many types of expression. The traditional idea that humans must act, or look, a certain way because others see them as either a "boy" or a "girl" stops people from being themselves.

You're probably asking yourself who made up the rules that teach us to treat each other differently based on our gender. For over 12,000 years, a system where gender roles are given to humans at birth has ruled the majority of countries, communities, and cultures. It is unfair, and positions men at an advantage, affecting how people of all genders are treated. Although this may be the norm worldwide, it doesn't make it the natural order of things or the standard that humanity is stuck with.

In the 18th century, **Olympe de Gouges** challenged the norms of her time by arguing that the "natural rights of man" should also be given to women. Her mindset conflicted with the majority of thinkers in her century, including German idealist **Georg Wilhelm Friedrich Hegel**, who was a controversial—but influential—figure in Western philosophy. His claim that "women's minds are not adapted to the higher sciences, philosophy, or certain of the arts" lines up with the worldview of his era. During Hegel's time, women in Western Europe were often forbidden from participating in life outside of the home.

We have come a long way since those days, but full equality will not happen as long as we are influenced by myths about how the differences in our bodies impact our ability. The impact of centuries' worth of discrimination is still felt today, too. Try to name the top five leaders you've learned about in school or on TV... If the first people who come to mind are men from Europe and North America, this has to do with who has historically been given the power and position to mold our education. This is why we need gender equality—or feminism—which is the belief in the social, economic, cultural, and political equality for people of all genders.

In a historical landscape where women were forced to stay at home, barred from access to media, and pushed out of schooling, women's voices were largely left out. Even though we know women were pondering the meaning of life and the world as far back as the 1st-century philosopher **Hypatia of Alexandria**, it took until the late 19th and 20th centuries for the voices of more women philosophers, such as **Simone de Beauvoir**, to emerge.

Although women in many societies have made historic gains over the past century, the movement for gender justice continues. Women, gender non-conforming people, and transgender people still face unequal treatment, representation, and access to resources.

"We teach girls to shrink themselves, to make themselves smaller. We say to girls, you can have ambition, but not too much. You should aim to be successful, but not too successful. Otherwise, you would threaten the man..."

– CHIMAMANDA NGOZI ADICHIE
(1977–) Nigerian feminist author

2

LIFE

WHY DO WE EXIST?

WHAT HAPPENS WHEN WE DIE?

WHAT IS HUMAN NATURE?

WHY DO WE LOVE?

WHY DO WE EXIST?

STRETCH YOUR ARMS IN FRONT OF YOU AND STARE AT YOUR HANDS FOR A MINUTE, SHARPENING YOUR GAZE WITH EVERY SECOND. Do you see an entire universe within the lines, freckles, pores, or colors on your skin?

If you have ever wondered why we exist, you're in good company!

Khalil Gibran, a Lebanese-American writer and artist, said "In one drop of water are found all the secrets of all the oceans; in one aspect of you are found all the aspects of existence." When we look at ourselves closely, we are reminded that we too are matter. Our cells are made up of atoms of elements such as hydrogen, carbon, nitrogen, and oxygen. We take up space like other living things that can be touched and seen. But does that mean that we're real? How did we get here? And what are we supposed to be doing?

If you have ever wondered why we exist, you're in good company! Across the globe, theorists, scientists, and spiritual leaders have done the same for thousands of years, debating questions and developing their ideas. Yes, the basic facts of how you came into the world are clear—through your biological parents, who were born because of your grandparents, who entered the world due to your great-grandparents, who emerged as a result of older ancestors. But there is more to the story.

Humanity's origin story differs depending on who you ask, but according to the laws of science everything that exists on Earth—including you—began as stardust. Scientists understand that the universe came into being about 13.8 billion years ago, with a grand explosion called the Big Bang. Nine billion years later, massive stars became so intensely hot and dense that they exploded, scattering parts across the universe that birthed the planets in our solar system—including our home, Earth.

Long before your earliest relatives took their first breath, the fiery force that created the stars and galaxies helped form every element in the periodic table, and life on our planet eventually took shape. As discussed on page 16, our current physical bodies came from a long process of change and adaptation that started from our earliest East African ancestors, primates who existed around 3 million years ago and evolved with the environment as they migrated worldwide.

Humans have pondered whether science, a higher power (or God), the environment, a "vital spark," or a mix of any of these ignited our being. Great thinkers from **Aristotle** and **Parmenides of Elea** to physicist **Stephen Hawking** have explored whether anything that existed before the forces that rocked the world into reality came from nothing... or something powerful.

Hawking said, "My goal is simple. It is a complete understanding of the universe, why it is as it is, and why it exists at all." **Edwin Hubble**, astronomer, had a similar thought: "Equipped with his five senses, man explores the universe around him and calls the adventure science."

"My goal is simple. It is a complete understanding of the universe, why it is as it is, and why it exists at all."

"The good thing about science is that it's true whether or not you believe in it."

NEIL deGRASSE TYSON
(1958-)
American scientist

23

WHAT HAPPENS WHEN

DO YOU REMEMBER WHAT YOU THOUGHT THE FIRST TIME YOU LEARNED ABOUT DEATH?

I stood still, closed my eyes, and held my breath when I overheard adults whispering about my great-grandmother's passing. As a child, I couldn't imagine why something as beautiful as life would ever end—at least in the form we'd known and enjoyed it.

When I thought about the idea that everything on Earth transitions and has a beginning and an end, my heart hurt. I feared the possibility that life as I knew it could change. Mostly, I didn't want to lose and miss the people, pets, or plants I loved growing up around. It was uncomfortable to think that death could not be altered like in a video game with a magic potion, or like it could be in my favorite storybooks.

"Mom and Dad, why can't people just press rewind like we do on a video?" I asked. After embracing me in a hug, my father responded, "Although every living thing passes one day, no one has ever come back to complain. Death, like anything, is a part of life. That's why it's important to make the time we have count and to always appreciate the people we care about."

For years, I took every chance to question adults about where our souls go when we die: what we do if we can't eat, move, or breathe, or whether we simply stop working, like a toy without a battery. It seemed that everyone had different ways of thinking and talking about a process just as human as being born.

> **"Death, like anything, is a part of life. That's why it's important to make the time we have count and to always appreciate the people we care about."**

WE DIE?

I felt that no one could tell me exactly what happens for sure, because none of us have experienced death yet. I asked myself whether I believed, like Ibn Sina, that the soul is separate from the body. Or whether I felt, as Epicurus taught, that death in itself is nothing to be scared of because it is the end of human awareness and fear.

> **"I died as a mineral and became a plant, I died as a plant and rose to animal, I died as an animal, and I was Man."**

Sometimes, I considered the view of the 13th-century Sufi Islamic philosopher **Rumi** who wrote that everything that lives will eventually be reborn. He said, "I died as a mineral and became a plant, I died as a plant and rose to animal, I died as an animal, and I was Man."

No matter what I heard, I noticed that most adults wanted to protect kids from the pain and grief that comes with loss. I also understood that they were careful about talking about death because they didn't have all the answers.

As I continue to explore what death means, I have found comfort in the fact that we're not alone in the experience of grief. Author **J. K. Rowling**'s wisdom that "things we lose have a way of coming back to us in the end, if not always in the way we expect" rings true when departed loved ones appear in dreams, memories, and feelings: the way we are reminded of how they lit up the world when we remember them. They may live on in the wisdom or lessons they left with us. As my mother said before she passed, "As long as you live, I am with you. In your DNA, in your cells, and in your heart. Love lives on."

WHAT IS HUMAN NATURE?

nature vs nurture

GOOD vs EVIL

REASON

IMAGINATION

emotion

THINK FOR A MOMENT ABOUT WHAT MAKES YOU HUMAN.

How do you know you are different from any other animal on Earth? Before you decide that this exercise seems silly—because you wouldn't even be doing it if you were a kitten or a kangaroo—consider the heart of this question.

For ages, thinkers have explored how we, as humans, are distinct from other animals, which have also evolved over time. Biological theories such as heredity explain how our emotions and actions have connections to the genes passed down by our ancestors, who adapted to their environment just as we continue to do today.

What makes humans distinct is our ability to reason, our drive to live together in community, and our powerful imaginations.

Many years before these scientific facts were common knowledge, Aristotle declared that what makes humans distinct from other animals is our ability to reason, our drive to live together in communities, and our powerful imagination. He also explored the idea that human nature is about finding meaning and purpose, which continues to be debated within many philosophical and spiritual spaces and is rooted in the question of whether we are driven by "nature" or "nurture."

The "nature vs. nurture" discussion considers whether we are *born with* the characteristics of human nature or whether *we are dependent on our surrounding environment* to help us develop our human nature over time. Most scientists and philosophers today understand the reality to be more complicated than just nature or just nurture.

Anthropologists have identified characteristics that all humans share beyond borders and cultures, like walking upright, using tools to prepare food, sharing and helping, adapting to changes in environment, and creating language and symbols to communicate. But some thinkers don't believe human nature exists at all. They point out the characteristics and behaviors we share with other animals—especially our ape ancestors. However, it's hard

PLATO

(428-348 BCE) ancient Greek philosopher

"To prefer evil to good is not in human nature; and when a man is compelled to choose one of two evils, no one will choose the greater when he might have the less."

to argue that humans are exactly the same as other primates. Apart from being tailless and less hairy than our primate relatives, humans have a more developed brain. The difference in the size of our brains contributes to how we speak, our higher level of self-awareness, and problem-solving skills. Studies have shown that humans and great apes can recognize themselves (and therefore their existence) in the mirror. But the type of consciousness we think about when it comes to making decisions about our sense of right and wrong involves a different experience of self-knowledge, beyond a simple understanding that a mirror shows us an image of ourselves.

The debate about whether it's human nature to be good, bad, moral, community-driven, or focused on the self is multilayered and depends on many factors, including culture and environment. What makes the most sense to you?

> **The debate about whether it's human nature to be good, bad, moral, community-driven, or focused on the self is multilayered.**

AGATHA CHRISTIE

(1890-1976) British author

"One always has hope for human nature."

ORSON WELLES

(1915-1985) American actor and writer

"Race hate isn't human nature; race hate is the abandonment of human nature."

NOAM CHOMSKY

(1928 –) American linguist

"Humans have certain properties and characteristics which are intrinsic to them, just as every other organism does. That's human nature."

SALMAN RUSHDIE

(1947–) British-Indian novelist

"I do think that there is such a thing as human nature, and that the things that we have in common are perhaps greater than the things that divide us."

CLOSE YOUR EYES AND THINK ABOUT SOMEONE YOU LOVE.

Is love a feeling, an experience, an action—or somewhere in between? Do you feel different types of love? If you painted a picture in your mind, what would someone viewing that image describe as your definition of love? Whether you experience love as a feeling, an action, a way of caring, or being thoughtful about the well-being of others, love means many things to different people.

Love can be shown in a variety of ways, including in our emotions, the ways we support each other, and the deeds we do in the world. It can be both joyful and painful if a relationship shifts. It can be an inspiring and motivating influence, while also making us fearful of the possibility that it may end.

No matter what our relationship to love is, love at its core is more complex than the romance we see in movies. For thousands of years, people have debated the nature of love and whether it is something that can—or even should—be measured. The ancient Greeks defined different types of love: *eros* (desire or passion for beauty in the form of people, ideas, and things), *philia* (appreciation, fondness, or devotion to your family, friends, community, pets, hobbies, and to ideas), and *agape* (loving and respecting all humanity, including yourself; some also interpret this as loving a higher power).

If you look at most philosophy that followed these ideas, including many aspects of diverse religious thinking from around the world, you'll find connections to these themes.

WHY DO WE LOVE

Many people believe in a scientific explanation for love—that it is something biology created to urge humans to procreate, and to form bonds that helped us live more successfully within communities. For some, love is a way we explain our attachment to desires. We can use it as an excuse to hang onto what we want, instead of being content with how things are. And for others, love is what humanizes us, brings us together, and helps us feel less alone in the world.

Love is a popular topic for scientists, artists, and philosophers to explore, with differing opinions about why we love and whether humans need love to thrive. The ancient Greek playwright **Sophocles** (sof-*uh*-kleez) taught that "One word frees us of all the weight and pain in life, that word is Love." **Lao Tzu** (lou-dzuh) thought that "Being deeply loved by someone gives you strength, while loving someone deeply gives you courage." **Voltaire** said, "Love is a canvas furnished by nature and embroidered by imagination." Mohandas (Mahatma) Gandhi said, "Where there is love there is life." And **bell hooks** reminds us that "Love is an action, never simply a feeling."

No matter what we think or who we are, love remains a mystery—although personal truths will unfold to us throughout our experience of life. Based on what you know already, or what you've seen, what does "love" mean to you?

> **"Where there is love there is life."**

"One word frees us of all the weight and pain in life, that word is Love."

SOPHOCLES
(496-406 BCE)
ancient Greek playwright/tragedian

29

3

TRUTH

IS GOD REAL?
WHAT IS TRUTH?
WHAT IS RIGHT AND WRONG?
WHAT IS JUSTICE?

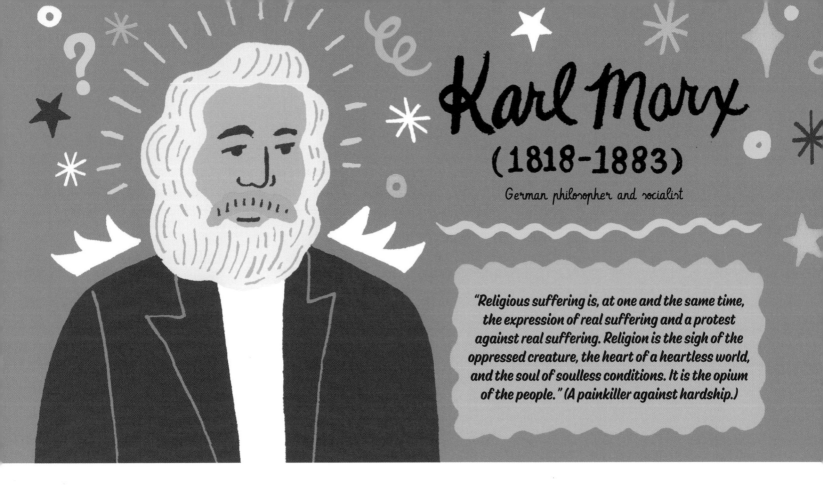

"Religious suffering is, at one and the same time, the expression of real suffering and a protest against real suffering. Religion is the sigh of the oppressed creature, the heart of a heartless world, and the soul of soulless conditions. It is the opium of the people." (A painkiller against hardship.)

IS GOD REAL?

I'LL NEVER FORGET WHEN ONE OF MY FRIENDS WHISPERED TO ME IN SUNDAY SCHOOL, "I'M AFRAID TO ASK MY PARENTS, BUT HOW DO WE KNOW THAT GOD IS REAL?" If this is a question you've asked yourself but been afraid to speak out loud, you're not alone. It was the first time that I'd thought about this question myself, because my family taught me to always put God first.

Years later, when a close friend told me that he'd asked his rabbi the same question during his bar mitzvah, I feared what he would say happened next. I was sure that he would get into trouble for questioning the existence of God in front of a religious leader. I based this on my experiences attending a Christian high school and growing up in Saudi Arabia, a country ruled by Islamic law. Instead, he surprised me

with the answer he had actually received. "Doubt is the foundation of faith," the rabbi had said to him, with a knowing grin.

I have thought about this exchange many times over the years, when I've bumped up against my own crises of faith. I've often wondered how to make sense of how the merciful, compassionate, and loving God in which I believe could allow atrocities such as racism, hatred, and war to happen. Now, I accept doubt as a pathway to learning about, and connecting with, spirituality. I'm sharing this story because the answers to this question are deeply personal— and can shift as we go through our lives.

Humans have been asking this question for generations, and there's no harm in asking questions to seek understanding. In the earliest religions, many people believed in the higher force of one single creator or multiple gods. As humanity began exploring

> **"Doubt is the foundation of faith."**

Maya Angelou
(1928–2014)
American author, poet, and activist

> "I found that I knew not only that there was God but that I was a child of God, when I understood that, when I comprehended that, more than that, when I internalized that, ingested that, I became courageous. If God loves me, if God made everything from leaves to seals and oak trees, then what is it I can't do?"

reason, humans began to ask more questions about whether it can be proved that a supreme being exists.

Aristotle taught that God is the one entity that was not created by something outside of itself. He thought that unlike human beings, who exist because our parents made us, God did not rely on any other being or force for its creation. Thinkers such as the Italian monk and philosopher **St. Anselm** argued that thinking about God proved God's existence, while the Italian friar **Thomas Aquinas** claimed, "God could have made the universe without humans and then made them." Centuries later, **Baruch Spinoza**, inspired by the medieval Jewish philosopher **Maimonides** (mahy-mon-i-deez), said that God is the cause of all things.

As time went on, more thinkers such as socialist philosopher **Karl Marx** disagreed, and argued that religion could be harmful: he described it as the "opium of the people," a drug used to control people who are dependent on the "illusions" it provides. Marx believed that religion is a painkiller against hardship: that the idea of God and an afterlife numbs the harsh reality of injustice. Some people feel sure, as Marx did, that there is nothing beyond this physical world. But others might perceive God as nature, or the force of science.

People who disbelieve in the idea that God or gods exist are atheists. Agnosticism is the belief that it's not possible to know or understand whether or not God or gods are real. Agnostics may or may not believe in God. Like any belief system, people relate to atheism and agnosticism in different ways. Some people are atheists because they were born into cultures where ideas about God were never spoken about. Others say that logic, science, and reason show proof that a God or gods are make-believe.

You might think of yourself as spiritual, religious, atheist, agnostic, humanist (someone who places more importance on humanity than on any divine power)—or not able to put a label on it. Wherever you land, exploring your own beliefs is a deeply personal journey, and no one has the right to judge or persecute you for what you do or do not believe.

WHAT IS TRUTH?

THINK ABOUT A TIME WHEN YOU HEARD SOMETHING THAT DIDN'T QUITE ADD UP FOR YOU.

It may have been a moment in which you encountered a friend stretching the truth with a light-hearted fib. Or perhaps you unearthed an outright lie in plain sight (like when a classmate stole my jacket and didn't give it back until we proved that the label sewed inside was my own.) Or it might have happened in the course of debating the Truth—with a capital "T"—about how our world, science, and species came to being.

Consider the questions that came to mind as soon as you realized you'd heard something that seemed false, impossible, or empty. Did asking questions help you figure out that what you were hearing wasn't true, right, or real? Or did the answers you were given result in even more things to be curious about?

Many great thinkers, including Socrates, believed that questions are the most important tools we can use to discover the truth. The idea is that by exploring questions through considering evidence, examples, and reasoned support for claims, we gain an understanding of what is real and accurate.

But throughout history, various governments, thinkers, media, and religious figures have debated whether people have a right to disagree with their understanding of the truth. They have disputed whether those in charge have the right to censor facts, withhold evidence, or control messages they disagree with.

Philosopher and free speech advocate Voltaire advised us to "Judge a man [person] by his questions rather than by his answers."

> "Judge a man by his questions rather than by his answers."

Although Voltaire and Socrates were separated by several centuries, they were both saying that the question is at the heart of our pursuit of the truth. So what does it mean if those in charge try to stop us from questioning?

Another idea that many philosophers have considered is how our identity, experiences, and education affect what we believe to be the truth. It's a human reality to acknowledge that we are all biased, or prejudiced, in certain ways—that is, we all favor some people and viewpoints over others, and make judgments based on our ideas of what is fair, right, good, or bad. Often, we are most biased toward ideas that mirror our own experiences and culture because of the beliefs, values, and assumptions we are taught at home, at school, in the media, and in our spiritual, philosophical, or religious traditions.

Are you biased? If you're breathing right now, the answer is yes!

So, are you biased? If you're breathing right now, the answer is yes! Ask yourself if you have ever had an opinion or feeling about something or someone without any real previous experience or knowledge. Ask yourself what you believe about the news, media, politicians, people from other countries or cultures, folks who practice different religions from yours, or people who have a gender that differs from the one you identify with.

How much of what you "know" is based on evidence and reason? What opinions might you have absorbed from different people and information sources in your community and living environment, without you even knowing it? It's important to notice when our reactions, and those of others, are driven by bias so we can interrupt harmful language and behavior when we hear or see it.

Now that you know that asking questions helps us discover the truth, does anything feel "off" to you in your life? Which ideas are you ready to explore or challenge?

WHAT IS RIGHT AND WRONG?

TAKE A MOMENT TO REFLECT ON HOW YOU LEARNED THE DIFFERENCE BETWEEN "GOOD" AND "BAD" ACTIONS. Chances are, you have a sense of which behaviors are helpful and which ones are harmful. Now, write down what you've learned about what's right and what's wrong in two columns.

Some thinkers, such as psychologist **Paul Bloom**, claim that we are born with a sense of right and wrong. He argues that infants are born with compassion and a sense of fairness. Many babies show their first sign of empathy when they attempt to ease others' suffering by patting or touching them. In an interview with *Scientific American*, he described babies' inborn connection with morality with a Thomas Jefferson quote "The moral sense is 'as much a part of a man as his leg or arm.'"

Throughout our youth, we learn from the adults around us (and in power) about which rules, laws, and policies we must follow to be considered "good" citizens. In most countries, governments decide the rules that shape societies. In governments where leaders are elected by the people to represent them, laws are meant to be framed around those people's needs.

Religious and spiritual ideas can also determine how people perceive right and wrong. Families and communities might decide how to live their lives based on their understanding of sacred texts, such as the Bible for Christians, the Torah for Jews, the Quran for Muslims, and the Vedas for Hindus.

The reality is that ideas about what is "right" or "wrong" are diverse and relative. They depend on our culture, history, background, and other factors. What is acceptable in one society may not be viewed as just or appropriate in another.

So does this mean that views and rules are "right", and should be followed, just because they

"An unjust law is no law at all." are coded into a society's law? **Dr. Martin Luther King, Jr.** addressed this, and the importance of activism in the face of unequal laws, in his famous "Letter from a Birmingham Jail." He wrote, "One has not only a legal but a moral responsibility to obey just laws. Conversely, one has a moral responsibility to disobey unjust laws. I would agree with **St. Augustine** that "an unjust law is no law at all." (Read more about justice on pages 38–39).

History, cultural attitudes, social movements, and timing affect when and how a culture changes its laws. For example, women won the right to vote in 1893 in New Zealand, in 1920 in the U.S.A., in 1928 in the U.K., and as recently as 2011 in Saudi Arabia (with limitations on full voting rights still in place now.) Connect this with the fact that although white women gained access to the vote in the U.S.A. in 1920, women of color—including Native American women and Black women—were held back from voting access by legal and social barriers until many years later.

Historically, many questions about "right" and "wrong" have been rooted in discussions about whether God and an afterlife exists (see pages 32–33): for example, are there everlasting consequences for our actions on Earth? Discussion also revolves around whether people have "free will"— the ability to choose their actions. If people can't make decisions freely, the idea is that their actions shouldn't be rewarded as "good" or judged as "bad."

In countries where laws came from Western philosophy, the law assumes that free will exists for all and that the courts will make judgments with this in mind. This is why laws related to children are often different, because questions arise about the extent to which people should be held responsible for their actions when their brains are still developing and they are still learning right from wrong.

You may be wondering whether some things are *always* simply right or wrong, no matter what the context. The Universal Declaration on Human Rights (read more about it on page 45) asserts that all human beings have a birthright to

certain "human rights" or freedoms throughout their lives, and that violating these rights is always wrong.

So, are people as responsible for actions we consider "wrong" if they are following the legal and moral values that their society sees as "right?" There were still people who opposed and fought the horrors of slavery when it was considered normal and legal. If people have free will to stand

against laws that violate people's rights, is it fair to judge them for not doing this? German philosopher **Immanuel Kant** said, "May you live your life as if the maxim of your actions were to become universal law." How do you want to live your life? What wrongs do you think should be made right in the world? What issues and injustices might future generations wonder why we let continue?

ANGELA DAVIS
(1944-)
American scholar, author, and activist

"I am no longer accepting the things I cannot change. I am changing the things I cannot accept."

NO

JUSTICE IS A HEAVY WORD. IT CARRIES THE WEIGHT OF ALL OUR HOPES AND DREAMS FOR WHAT IT COULD MEAN FOR OUR SOCIETY, BOTH NOW AND IN THE FUTURE.

WHAT

Depending on whom you ask, justice has different meanings. For some, it's simply about the letter of the law. For others, it is about values, morals, culture, and ideals. In many cases, people view justice as a combination of all these things.

The ancient Greeks talked a lot about the meaning of justice. Plato noted their different views down in a book called *The Republic*. **Thrasymachus** (*thras-imi-cuss*) thought that those who have power should get to decide what is right and wrong. He thought justice is the advantage of being on top. However, Socrates and Plato didn't think that was so smart. Plato responded, "Do not expect justice where might is right." Here, he is saying that justice should not be based purely on the brute force of those in power: it should be based on harmony.

Thousands of years later, debates about justice are still timely and important. How do we define justice? What inspires people to behave in a just way? Is justice a good thing? What are its benefits and punishments for people? How do we determine when we've achieved justice, when so many people see it so differently?

Personally, I understand justice as a living and breathing organism, much more than just a collection of written laws and codes. It is also about

IS

access, opportunity, community, partnership, and action.

I started thinking about my own definition of justice when I attended my first protest at around eight years old. I joined my family to challenge the unjust firing of a Black educator who spoke truth to power in our small, traditional, and conservative hometown.

I have a snapshot of myself marching in between my parents, in a sea of other Brown faces, etched into my mind. This memory marks my activist awakening. That night, my mom asked if I had any questions about what I witnessed. I muttered, "Mommy, I just can't understand how racism still exists if we have laws that say we are equal now."

I didn't understand why someone would lose their job for trying to push for change that would make things better for everyone in the community, rather than a select, fortunate few. After all, one of my teachers told me that we had the right to free speech, and that the unfair times in which my parents grew up were over long ago. I'd also heard similar messages in the news— which was confusing, because I also noticed bias (see page 35) on those same channels. Mom sighed, "Baby, just because we have laws it doesn't mean everything is fair or just. The law to end <u>segregation</u> in schools was passed years before I graduated from an all-Black high school. Justice

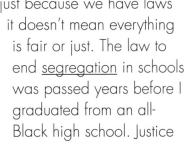

"I just can't understand how racism still exists if we have laws that say we are equal now."

JUSTICE?

is possible only if the government and culture shapes laws that are fair and apply to everyone. If the people who decide the laws aren't as diverse as the people who are ruled by them, you probably don't have justice."

She went on to explain that although laws and policies that are moral, fair, and within reach for everyone are the goal, history has proven that they aren't always the reality. She also shared what was, for me, the most important part of the lesson—that fairness is not always the same as justice, particularly when one group of people are historically disadvantaged: "The people in charge when I was young told us that our schools would be 'separate but equal,' but that was far from the truth."

As I reflect on the path I took toward becoming an activist, in my life and career, I often return to this flashback with my mom, the spark that lit up my desire for social justice work. She taught me that we must all do our part to advance justice—and it is never too early to start.

> **"Fairness is not the same as justice."**

In the face of injustice, I often ask myself what justice might look, sound, and feel like. Next, I challenge myself to think about how I could take one step to get closer to making it a reality. And then another. And then one more. And then invite someone to join me. And then another…until we arrive at justice or as close as we possibly can.

What kind of justice are you seeking? How might you get there?

Benjamin Franklin

1706-1790

American politician

"Justice will not be served until those who are unaffected are as outraged as those who are."

Elie Wiesel

1928-2016

Romanian writer and Nobel Laureate

"There may be times when we are powerless to prevent injustice, but there must never be a time when we fail to protest."

Gloria E. Anzaldúa

1942-2004

American scholar

"Nothing happens in the 'real' world unless it first happens in the images in our heads."

Cornel West

1953-

American philosopher and author

"Never forget that justice is what love looks like in public."

4

CULTURE

WHAT IS IMAGINATION?
WHAT IS FREEDOM?
IS AN IDEAL SOCIETY POSSIBLE?
WHAT IS KNOWLEDGE?

WHAT IS IMAGINATION?

OUR IMAGINATION GIVES US THE FREEDOM TO EXPLORE ENDLESS POSSIBILITIES WITHOUT ANY LIMITS. It is a powerful and useful part of the mind that allows us to expand our horizons, and envision new pathways or potential realities.

Our imaginations are alive, fluid, open, and full of possibility if we allow ourselves to play, make new things, and explore fresh ideas. Growing up, I relied on my imagination to feed my curiosity and to act as an anchor that brought me back to the sanctuary of my own nature, thoughts and dreams. It helped me feel safe, confident, and free whenever someone told me I couldn't do or say something because I was a girl, or because I was born with a disability. It provided comfort and healing, while also offering me ways to tap into my strengths, embrace my dreams, and accept myself. As **Muhammad Ali** said, "The [person] who has no imagination has no wings."

When physicist **Albert Einstein** said "imagination is more important than knowledge," he understood that knowledge could be gained with time and practice, but imagination is the fire that fuels creativity and change. He argued that we can't "solve our problems with the same thinking we used when we created them," calling on us to apply both reason and imagination when asking and answering big questions.

> **"Imagination is more important than knowledge."**

Imagination is about world-making. It helps us understand ourselves and everything outside of us with a fresh perspective. That's why humans connect deeply with storytelling, fantasy, and lore (traditional stories and knowledge). American science-fiction writer **Octavia E. Butler** acknowledged the importance of pairing knowledge with creativity to capture imaginations through her work: "Fantasy is totally wide open; all you really have to do is follow the rules you've set. But if you're writing about science, you have to first learn what you're writing about."

> **Imagination is about world-making.**

Although many great minds have insisted on the importance of imagination, practices in our schools and the workplace don't always mirror this mindset. British educator **Ken Robinson** has spoken about how we are born with creativity and "get educated out of it." He argues that being imaginative is as important as being able to read and write, but that schools currently focus on training children to be good, obedient workers, rather than encouraging their creativity and diverse ways of thinking.

Robinson's belief that "imagination is the source of all human achievement" is at the heart of the imagination-led "learning revolution" that he wants to see take place in schools and beyond.

What do you think? How might we use our imagination to grow at school and beyond?

"The power of imagination created the illusion that my vision went much farther than the naked eye could actually see."

NELSON MANDELA (1918–2013)
South African president and activist

WHAT IS FREEDOM?

FREEDOM MEANS MORE THAN BEING ABLE TO DO OR FEEL WHAT WE WANT. Depending on whom you ask, it has many different names and definitions. But no matter how we understand it, freedom is about power.

You might be wondering, "What kind of power?" Freedom allows us to speak, move, think, act, and make choices based on our own free will. But what happens when one person's freedom starts to impact on another's? Some see freedom as a state of being completely free from any outside forces or laws at all, to do what they wish. For others, freedom means having rules and guidelines that allow each of us to flourish without unjust or biased limits. For many, it's a mix of these. All of us have our own unique take on how being free looks and feels, and yet some elements of freedom—such as human rights and liberty—should be universal. Have you given any thought to what you think of as freedom?

As a child, I often wondered how freedom was connected with its close sibling, justice (see pages 38–39). It started when I asked my teacher to explain why "liberty and justice" are named together in the U.S. <u>Pledge of Allegiance</u> we recited each morning at school in South Carolina. Every morning, we placed our hands on our hearts and said in unison, "I pledge allegiance to the Flag of the United States of America and to the Republic for which it stands, one nation under God, indivisible, with liberty and justice for all." My teacher explained that the state of being "free" is supported when a nation's laws are just and fair for all people.

Although we spoke of freedom and equality in the pledge, I knew laws don't always stop bias, <u>bigotry</u>, or discrimination. And, even if they did, folks with less access to information or money to get legal support were left under-served by them. I felt disappointed. One day, I asked if I could be excused from saying the pledge because I didn't believe that it was a reality for everyone—yet. I was also curious about why God was mentioned. We had been told that the U.S.A. created its "separation of church and state" laws to protect freedom of thought and religion. Although I'm a Christian who believes in God, it didn't make sense to me based on what we had learned.

My teacher's face reddened when I uttered these words. He replied with a question that roared like a demand, "Well, you wouldn't want anyone to think you're not patriotic—don't you love your country? I'm going to talk to your parents about this."

My ankles shook while I told him that I'd read the history of our laws and I understood that my right to speak freely was what freedom and patriotism were all about. I replied, "What if I asked these questions because I love my country and I want to get to a point where these words are true for everyone? Also, I looked it up and standing silent or sitting during the pledge counts as free speech." My heartbeat quickened, but I straightened up tall as I shared my truth.

My teacher called my mom to report my behavior and was shocked when she supported, rather than punished, me. From that day forward, I was allowed to stand for the pledge without saying anything. Although my family never told me that I shouldn't say the pledge, they believed in my freedom to question. I'm forever grateful that they didn't block my journey of discovery because being able to explore my own understanding of freedom helped me become the activist I am today. My experience at school inspired me to search for how we came to define and understand freedom. I discovered that freedom has many pathways, including freedom of thought, freedom of expression, freedom of the press, freedom of speech, freedom of religion, freedom to pursue happiness, and freedom of movement. In theory, these laws exist to defend against unfairness and discrimination based on someone's gender, race, disability, age, birthplace, and so on. But they also set the tone for cultural and moral ideas about equality and community.

I read about thinkers such as Voltaire and John Stuart Mill, who argued that we're all entitled to free speech in both the spoken and written word. I learned about the long tradition of protest that helped shape the U.S.A., from the proclamation of American independence to the major events of the <u>civil rights</u> movement.

I also became fascinated by the United Nations' Universal Declaration of Human Rights, which was adopted in 1948. In addition to setting the mold for laws in many new <u>democracies</u>, this document made history by stating that essential human rights should be universally protected.

People with different cultures, languages, and viewpoints created the text that declared, "All humans are born free, and equal in dignity and rights. They are endowed with reason and conscience and should act towards one another in a spirit of brotherhood." Although I would change "brotherhood" to "humanity" to include all of us, these ideas helped me develop my own thinking about freedom. What does freedom mean to you?

IS AN IDEAL SOCIETY POSSIBLE?

TAKE A MOMENT TO DREAM ABOUT YOUR VISION FOR A BETTER WORLD.
What does your ideal world look like? Have you ever really thought about what it would feel like to live in a free and just community and culture?

When I was 13 years old, my idea of <u>utopia</u>, or a perfect world, formed during long road trips with my family. As we crisscrossed the Eastern seaboard of the U.S.A. every summer, I filled the hours on the road with visions of an idyllic new reality. Bathing in the breeze from riding with the windows down, I read books about idealist societies on Earth or in space. I closed my eyes tightly while humming along with songs like my dad's favorite, **John Lennon**'s "Imagine," on repeat.

Something about these cheerful stretches on the open road kept me focused on possibilities and a brighter future. I longed to live in these moments forever. Firing up the ignition always meant that I'd have a long stint of time to daydream—or "Imagine"—what it would take to create the best type of society. Going somewhere with my loved ones always expanded my sense of being and safety in the world.

A few years later, I found an entry about my "dream society" in one of my tattered old diaries. As I turned the pages of memories, poems, watercolors, and short stories, I recalled the adventures I escaped into during our journeys. While each page told a different story, they were tied together by themes such as freedom, justice, love, knowledge, dignity, and equality for all people. I fantasized about a perfect imaginary world that lifted people up, championed art, outlawed bullying, celebrated difference, valued education, and cared for people. After re-reading my journal, I wondered if a society like this had to be a work of fiction. I then considered whether I'd been taught by culture and social systems that a truly just society was unrealistic or naïve.

What would it take for us to live in a state of mind, a sense of place, and an environment that is truly healthy and safe for everyone? During debates in the school classroom, I learned that humanity had long been exploring the idea of a perfect world—and that our own versions of utopia tended to match up with those of philosophers whose experiences are closer to ours.

Some of us in the class identified with Socrates' conversation in Plato's *Republic* about a multi-gender city-state ruled by philosopher guardians. Others connected more to **Amerigo Vespucci**'s (*uh*-**mer**-i-goh ve-**spoo**-chee) vision of a lawless state where people "live in perfect liberty and have neither king nor lord."

Although my vision for the world includes all people, I was interested in 15th-century writer **Christine de Pizan**'s women-only utopia. It helped pave the way for future conversations in my life about gender equality and feminism.

Books such as *Gulliver's Travels, Brave New World, Walden Two*, and Octavia E. Butler's *Parable of the Sower* taught me that although a better world is possible, the meaning of utopia in Greek—"no place"—is fitting. Is utopia possible when everyone has a different idea of what makes a perfect world? Perhaps our goal is to determine how to focus on creating solutions that solve issues we face now, so that generations in the future will benefit.

Thinking about the possibility of utopia throws up all sorts of complex questions. Do all humans really want to exist in a state where everyone shares everything and is on the same level in society? How does culture affect how we imagine what the best form of society is? Can we reach a shared understanding of what utopia means if we want or need different things? And, finally, can we create a perfect community if we're not perfect beings?

> "Live in perfect liberty and have neither king nor lord."

EVERY ONE OF US KNOWS A LOT OF THINGS. We might even take some of them for granted—such as how to count, or that grass is green and the sky is blue. But have you ever stopped to think about how you learned all of it? How did these ideas become what you now "know" to be true?

Knowledge is usually defined as thoughts that are rooted in facts, supported by logic, and useful to humankind. We can gain education from information that is passed on to us at home, at school, or through other experiences. For example, I learned basic American Sign Language when I was a child because my parents worked with children who were deaf and hard of hearing. When our class was taught how to sign the alphabet in school, I already knew how. I had figured out how to sign from watching my friends and family use sign language at my parents' clinic.

On pages 10–11 and 34–36, we've looked at discussions about how we know who we are and how we understand "truth". So what does it mean to *know* something? There are many ways that scientists and other thinkers understand knowledge, depending on their point of view. For example, Aristotle believed that humans can understand every aspect of our world, starting with ourselves. He said, "Knowing yourself is the beginning of all wisdom."

Aristotle valued awareness and insisted that we gain knowledge from what we observe in nature through our senses—sight, hearing, taste, smell, and touch. He applied this approach in studying every subject available to him, including biology, zoology, weather, astronomy, and geography.

Over time, we have expanded how we

WHAT

IS

KNOWLEDGE?

think about building our knowledge. In the 1990s, African-American feminist scholar bell hooks—along with other female thinkers of color, such as **Cherríe Moraga**—sought to honor and recognize the power of diverse ways of knowing. In the Western world, knowledge that can be "proven" through science is usually considered more important, or trustworthy, than other types of knowledge. But hooks argued that knowledge does not require scientific research to be valid, and can be rooted in "experience" and love, and felt in the body. She said, "Knowledge rooted in experience shapes what we value and as a consequence, how we know what we know as well as how we use what we know." Can you think of something you know that can't be scientifically proven, but through your experience you are sure of?

More recently, Indian educational researcher and 2013 TED Prize winner **Sugata Mitra** made waves when he declared that "knowledge is obsolete" and claimed that young people have a natural sense of wisdom that grows when supported and encouraged through child-led learning, rather than learning by memorizing or repetition. I met Sugata when I was working at TED (who organize and post their "TED talks" online). He transformed the way I thought about what I know, and how I came to understand my own thinking.

Mitra has carried out research with young people in different countries, across various social and economic lines. In these studies he found that one pattern remained the same from the U.K. to India: young people will teach themselves, and each other, when they are inspired by the natural fire of curiosity, receiving support from encouraging, caring adults, and building a community with their peers.

Leonardo Da Vinci
1452-1519

Italian inventor, painter, and polymath

"Nature is the source of all true knowledge. She has her own logic, her own laws, she has no effect without cause nor invention without necessity."

Francis Bacon
1561-1626

English philosopher and politician

"Knowledge is power."

Marcus Garvey
1887-1940

Jamaican activist, publisher, and orator

"A people without the knowledge of their past history, origin and culture is like a tree without roots."

Barbara McClintock
1902-1992

American scientist and Nobel Laureate

"If you know you are on the right track, if you have this inner knowledge, then nobody can turn you off ... no matter what they say."

Don Miguel Ruiz
1952-

Mexican spiritual teacher and author

"Humans believe so many lies because we aren't aware. We ignore the truth or we just don't see the truth. When we are educated, we accumulate a lot of knowledge, and all that knowledge is just like a wall of fog that doesn't allow us to perceive the truth, what really is."

Malala Yousafzai
1997-

Pakistani education activist and Nobel laureate

"One child, one teacher, one book, one pen can change the world."

5

CREATIVITY

WHAT IS BEAUTY?

WHAT IS MEMORY?

WHAT IS A SOUL?

WHAT IS YOUR BIGGEST

QUESTION OR IDEA?

WHAT IS BEAUTY?

What immediately comes to mind? Is beauty something you see, feel, hear, touch, or experience through all of your senses? Do you find the same things beautiful that other people do? Or, are you sometimes attracted to art, music, or parts of nature that other people describe as ugly?

> **Is beauty something you see, feel, hear, touch, or experience through all of your senses?**

When I think of beauty, I recall the first time I saw a rainbow after an unexpected winter snowfall. The brilliantly colored arc in the sky captured my attention as the frost melted into mirror-like puddles on the ground. My grandma Georgia, my mother, and my friend from pre-school gazed at our reflections in the puddle-mirrors. We marveled at what looked like mini-rainbows on our faces. The sounds of their laughter jingled like a wind chime, comforting me in a way that made me want to make that moment and our togetherness last forever, and ever.

This snapshot in my mind reminds me of *The Color Purple*, a movie based on a book by feminist author **Alice Walker**. The central character, Celie, said that she thought God got upset "if you walk by the color purple in a field somewhere and don't notice it." After seeing the movie, I always stopped to breathe in and witness beauty whenever and wherever I could.

I thought of this, years later, when my teacher asked us to write about the first thing we found attractive, lovely, or "aesthetically" pleasing. She explained that "aesthetic" means to be concerned with beauty, or our appreciation or perception of beauty through our senses. It's also a kind of thinking that explores the nature of art, beauty, and our taste for what is appealing.

The teacher asked us all to think about what makes something beautiful. She said, "I'm sure you've heard that 'beauty is in the eye of the beholder.' I want you to draw the experiences you wrote about... then ask your classmates about whether they think it is beautiful or not."

I shivered at the mention of this assignment. I was OK at art, but drawing wasn't my strong suit. I trusted my teacher, though, and felt inspired when she read out a quote from artist **Henri Matisse** who said, "Creativity takes courage." As we passed our art around the room, I tried to keep an open mind and a trusting attitude.

As my classmates and I shared our opinions about each other's visions of beauty, we quickly realized that we had both similar and different ways of seeing the world. One of my schoolmates suggested that I could have drawn my rainbows with the exact colors that appear in the scientific spectrum. I told her the reason my sketch used different tones was that I drew what I felt I remembered into the work, too.

Others thought the story of that snowy day could have been more powerful if I drew the image in black and white with pencils. They supported a vision that would have left the colors to the viewer's imagination. The teacher said we were all correct. She asked us, "Does it make the image of your experience with beauty any less true because you understand it differently to someone else? Do you both need to value it the same way for it to matter?" She soon explained that she was leading us down a path that philosophers have traveled for ages, exploring ideas about beauty.

She used our exercise as an example of the kinds of questions philosophers such as Immanuel Kant and David Hume explored about art and beauty.

Kant thought experiencing beauty was much like tasting something: you know immediately if the ice cream is delicious, without thinking about it. But at the same time, beauty was pure: it doesn't fulfill a need, like hunger, so we do not have the same interest in it. It is not linked to our moral judgement and it is not linked to facts. We are distanced from it.

Hume's view was that we base our thoughts about beauty on our personal opinions and taste. To Hume, there's no correct answer to the question of what is beautiful since our own individual perspectives influence how we judge beauty.

Even if many of us agree that something is beautiful, someone might react to that thing differently, based on their viewpoints or experiences. This is the gorgeous upside to creative subjects. We all see beauty differently.

> **"Do you both need to value it the same way for it to matter?"**

"Beauty and ugliness are a mirage, because others always end up seeing what's inside us."

FRIDA KAHLO
1907-1954
Mexican painter

WHAT IS MEMORY?

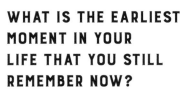

WHAT IS THE EARLIEST MOMENT IN YOUR LIFE THAT YOU STILL REMEMBER NOW?

For most of us, our earliest memory is from between the ages of three and four years old. Some of us might recall things that happened when we were two, but it is rare. Science shows that our ability to form memories doesn't fully develop in the earliest "pre-verbal" stage of life.

Some of our most vivid memories might not have happened exactly the way we think they did, either. Scientists have found that the words we use to recall an event can actually influence what we believe happened at that time.

Author **John Kotre** describes how our brain has a way of rewriting the past, turning good things in our history into perfect memories, and sometimes magnifying bad experiences as even worse than they were. This is no cause for worry, just a fact that helps us understand why something might feel real and true, but is also impacted by our biases (see page 35).

When I was younger, my family often teased me about my elephant-like memory. My ability to retain information was useful when it came to pop quizzes at school or trivia nights. However, the flip side was that it could also cause conflict with others who didn't remember things the way I did.

Relationships sometimes became strained when I harped on with detailed explanations I remembered long after my parents, friends, or teachers forgot them. The same mind that made late-night studying for tests easy also made it difficult to erase even the tiniest details of painful memories or disagreements.

Often, bitterness followed when I pointed out something that folks around me wanted to forget or pretend didn't happen. I learned over and over that sometimes people will do anything to stop you bringing up something that they want to sweep under the rug.

My memory has been best defined by what a fortune-teller in New Orleans told me, upon first laying eyes on me: "Gal, you are so sweet and kind, but what most don't know is that, for you, it's never easy to forgive. Why? Because you don't forget a thing."

Humans are still exploring how to understand fully the power of our memory. Still, there's a lot we do know. For example, a small part of your brain called the hippocampus—named because of its shape after the Greek word for "seahorse"— forms, arranges, and stores your memories.

It is also where you link your memories and emotions together, and shape your long-term memories. Like a seahorse-shaped compass, the hippocampus helps us find our way and influences our emotional responses. One reason it's important to limit stress in our lives is that it can cause the sensitive hippocampus to become inflamed. Damage to this vital part of the brain can affect our ability to recall older memories or properly form new ones.

Philosophers such as John Locke thought about how memory connects with our

HIPPOCAMPUS
(MEMORY)

sense of self and identity. Locke claimed that what makes us who we are now is the fact that we can recall what happened before. For him, our memory defines who we are: our personalities are the sum of our experiences and memories. More recently, psychologists have critiqued this idea, as research shows that we tend to pick and choose our memories when creating our personal narratives. For example, someone who thinks of themselves as a confident person will more easily remember situations where they have acted confidently, than when they haven't.

What do you think? Do our memories make us all have different ideas? What role does our memory play in defining who we are?

What role does our memory play in defining who we are?

WHAT IS A SOUL?

WHAT DOES THE WORD 'SOUL' MEAN TO YOU? For me, your soul is your essence. It is the spirit within a living being that is energetic. Depending on what you believe, the soul is often associated with our mind, memory, and sense of self.

Our own cultural, historic, religious, and spiritual viewpoints influence how we understand this part of ourselves and others. In many spiritual, cultural, and philosophical traditions, the soul represents a state of being that is not part of your material body.

The soul of someone or something might also be described as its heart, breath, core, or consciousness. When someone speaks of a book, home, space, place, or a community as "having a soul," they are referring to the most important or essential part of something. When I describe someone as "soulful," it means that I regard them as someone who feels deeply and is connected with their true human nature.

Humans have thought about souls for thousands of years. There is proof that prehistoric cultures and ancient Chinese and Egyptian traditions believed in a soul that exists beyond our mortal bodies.

Other ancient cultures, such as the early Hebrews, thought of the soul as something not separate from the body—although this concept later evolved in Judaism. Some ancient Greeks believed in a separate body and soul, which later influenced Christian bishops such as St. Augustine, and followers of Plato viewed the soul as spiritual, rather than physical, and immortal. Some philosophers, such as Descartes, saw the soul and the mind as essentially the same thing. Others, such as **William James**, doubted the existence of the soul entirely and instead chalked it up to what he called "psychic phenomena."

In Hinduism, the soul is also described as breath. It is thought to be eternal, but stuck in a mortal body when we're born. It goes on to enter a cycle of death and rebirth that is determined by karma—or the collective results of our deeds. Most followers of Christian and Islamic traditions believe that the individual soul is born when the body is, but lives on beyond the body. Buddhism, on the other hand, sees the idea of an individual eternal soul as an illusion.

The concept of the soul is usually a spiritual conversation rather than a scientific one. But some experiments in quantum theory point to the possibility of the mind being limitless in time and space.

> The concept of the soul is usually a spiritual conversation rather than a scientific one.

Other thinkers like writer **Aaron Freeman** argue that energy, not souls live on. According to Freeman, the first law of thermodynamics proves that once energy is formed in the universe it can't be or ended. He supported his claims with the law of the conservation of energy and stated that people should ask physicists to speak at their memorial services to explain that the particles, heat, and neurons that made them human will remain beyond their death. He said, "Not a bit of you is gone; you're just less orderly."

What do you believe? Read these ideas from thinkers who represent a variety of mindsets to decide where you stand.

VOLTAIRE

(1694-1778)

French thinker and writer

"Nobody thinks of giving an immortal soul to a flea."

HELEN KELLER

(1880-1968)

American author and activist

"Character cannot be developed in ease and quiet. Only through experience of trial and suffering can the soul be strengthened, ambition inspired, and success achieved."

LANGSTON HUGHES

(1902-1967)

American writer

"My soul has grown deep like the rivers."

THICH NHAT HANH

(1926-)

Vietnamese Buddhist monk and peace activist

"You don't need a soul, or a self, in order to continue. It's like a cloud. Even when the cloud is not there, it continues always as snow or rain. The cloud does not need to have a soul in order to continue. There's no beginning and no end. You don't need to wait until the total dissolution of this body to continue—you continue in every moment."

DEEPAK CHOPRA

(1946-)

American author

"Trust that your soul has a plan, and even if you can't see it completely, know that everything will unfold as it is meant to."

MEGGAN WATTERSON

(1974 -)

American theologian and writer

"Are you loving you? Are you hearing the voice of love within you, your soul-voice, and believing it enough to act on its directives? This is what the practice of loving ourselves looks like: we do whatever we have to do to hear our soul's voice and believe it. We believe it so much that we make our life about that encounter."

WHY?

WHAT IS YOUR QUESTION

WE'VE COME TO THE END OF THIS BOOK BUT IT'S JUST THE START OF YOUR PHILOSOPHIZING ADVENTURES.

Now it's time to take what you've learned and use it to help you think creatively about your own big questions and ideas.

Are there ideas that keep you up at night? What questions do you wish you could learn more about? What's your big "why?"—or your big "how?" Is there a vision you have for the world that you haven't written or spoken about yet? Connect with others and ask away!

TIMELINE

Lao Tzu
Taoist
601–531BCE

Siddhartha Gautama (Buddha)
sage, philosopher, teacher and religious leader
563–483BCE

Confucius
philosopher and politician
551–479BCE

Parmenides of Elea
philosopher
515BCE–unknown

Sophocles
tragedian/ playwright
497–406BCE

Baruch Spinoza
philosopher
1632–1677

René Descartes
philosopher, mathematician, and scientist
1596–1650

Amerigo Vespucci
explorer
1454–1512

Christine de Pizan
author and poet
1364–c.1430

Thomas Aquinas
Catholic friar
1225–1274

John Locke
philosopher and physician
1632–1704

Voltaire
thinker and writer
1694–1778

David Hume
philosopher, historian, economist, and essayist
1711–1776

Immanuel Kant
philosopher
1724–1804

Olympe de Gouges
playwright and political activist
1748–1793

Shirley Chisholm
politician, educator, and author
1924–2005

Simone de Beauvoir
writer and philosopher
1908–1986

Frida Kahlo
painter
1907–1954

e.e. cummings
poet and painter
1894–1962

Edwin Hubble
astronomer
1889–1953

Maya Angelou
author, poet and activist
1928–2014

Noam Chomsky
linguist
1928–

Dr. Martin Luther King, Jr.
civil rights activist and baptist minister
1929–968

Gloria Steinem
feminist writer and activist
1934–

Marge Piercy
poet and novelist
1936–

bell hooks
feminist author
1952–

Ken Robinson
author, speaker and advisor on education in the arts
1950–

Salman Rushdie
novelist
1947–

Octavia E. Butler
author
1947–2006

Sugata Mitra
professor
1952–

Don Miguel Ruiz
author of Toltec spiritualist and neoshamanistic texts
1952–

Cherríe Moraga
Chicana activist and writer
1952–

Robin DiAngelo
academic, lecturer, and author
1956–

Socrates
philosopher
470–399BCE

Thrasymachus
sophist (a kind of teacher)
459–400BCE

Plato
philosopher
428–348BCE

Aristotle
philosopher
384–322BCE

Epicurus
philosopher and sage
341–270BCE

St. Augustine
Christian theologian
AD354–430

Rumi
poet, faqih, Islamic scholar, theologian, and Sufi mystic
1207–1273

Maimonides
philosopher
1135–1204

St. Anselm
philosopher
1033–1109

Ibn Sina
physician, astronomer, thinker and writer
980–1037

Hypatia of Alexandria
philosopher, astronomer, and mathematician
370–415

Georg Wilhelm Friedrich Hegel
philosopher
1770–1831

Alexis de Tocqueville
diplomat and historian
1805–1859

John Stuart Mill
philosopher and economist
1806–1873

Karl Marx
philosopher and socialist
1818–1883

William James
psychologist and philosopher
1842–1910

Ludwig Wittgenstein
philosopher
1889–1951

Khalil Gibran
writer and artist
1883–1931

Albert Einstein
physicist
1879–1955

Mohandas (Mahatma) Ghandi
activist
1869–1948

Henri Matisse
painter, draughtsman, printmaker, and sculptor
1869–1954

Judy Chicago
artist
1939–

John Lennon
singer, songwriter and peace activist
1940–1980

John Kotre
author and professor
1940–

Gloria E. Anzaldúa
scholar
1942–2004

Stephen Hawking
physicist
1942–2018

Alice Walker
feminist author
1944–

Angela Davis
scholar, author, and activist
1944–

Muhammad Ali
champion boxer and pacifist
1942-2016

Aaron Freeman
writer and commentator
1956–

Neil deGrasse Tyson
scientist
1958–

J. K. Rowling
writer
1965–

Paul Bloom
psychologist
1963–

GLOSSARY

activist—a person who campaigns to create political or social change.

agnostic—a person who believes that nothing is known or can be known about whether God exists or has a state of being. It can also mean a person who claims neither faith nor disbelief in God.

ancestors—people in your family who were born before you. People who you are descended from.

atheist—a person who does not believe that God exists.

anthropologist—scientists who study human societies.

bar mitzvah—the religious coming of age ceremony for a Jewish boy who has reached the age of 13 and is regarded as ready to observe religious teachings and take part in public worship. Bat mitzvahs are the coming of age ceremony girls participate in at 13.

bias or biased—prejudice for or against a thing, person, or group, often in an unjust way.

bigotry—intolerance towards people who have a different opinion or way of life.

censor or **censorship**—to examine a publication, music, or a work of art and block others from experiencing it.

civil rights—the rights of people in a community to access freedom and equality.

Civil Rights Movement—a mass protest for social justice for African Americans to gain equal rights under US law.

colonialism—the policy or practice of taking control over another country, inhabiting it with settlers, and profiting from it economically.

democracy—a system of government where every person has a say in how their government is run by using their vote as their voice.

discrimination—the unjust or biased treatment of different people based on religion, race, age, disability, sex, nationality, or immigration status.

feminism—advocacy for gender justice on the basis of equality for all people.

free will—the power of acting without being controlled by fate; the ability to act based on our own decisions.

friar—a member of any of specific religious orders of men within the Catholic Church.

gender—an array of identities, roles, codes, and ways of being culture teaches us to adhere to; gender identity and expression is about who you understand yourself to be.

gender non-conforming—people who do not conform to stereotypical social norms or expectations about how they should identify or behave related to their perceived gender.

genetic/genes—relating to genes or heredity.

heredity—the passing on of physical or mental traits genetically from one generation to another.

hippocampus—the long ridges on each lateral ventricle of the brain, thought to be the center of emotion, memory, and the autonomic nervous system.

humanist—a follower of the principles of humanism, which is a way of thinking that stresses the value of humanity, human needs, and solutions to social and cultural issues.

human rights—a right that must belong justly to every person.

Indigenous—original ethnic groups, owners, and caretakers of a region that has been colonized by outsiders.

karma—(in Hinduism and Buddhism) the sum of a person's actions in this and previous states of being, viewed as deciding their fate in future forms of life.

lineage—a person's family line; ancestry or pedigree.

matter—a physical substance.

maxim—a short statement expressing truth or a rule of conduct.

periodic table—a chemical chart of the elements.

philosophy—the study of the nature of knowledge, reality, and existence.

Pledge of Allegiance—an expression of allegiance to the flag of the United States and the republic of the United States of America.

polymath—someone who has a lot of knowledge about many subjects.

prejudice—dislike, anger, or unjust behavior against people from another community or who have ideas that differ from one's own.

quantum theory—a scientific theory of matter and energy.

rabbi—a Jewish scholar or teacher who studies and teaches Jewish law.

race—the non-scientific idea that human beings belong to different groups based on inherited physical traits or features.

segregation—to keep one group of people apart from another and treat them differently, especially because of race.

socialist—a person who advocates or practices socialism. Socialism is a system where the government controls how goods are distributed among the people. Businesses are owned by workers and the people who depend on the goods they create.

stereotype—a widely held but simplistic image or idea of what a specific type of person or thing is like.

transgender—relating to a person whose gender identity is not the same as the one they were assigned at birth.

utopia—a sense of place or a state of being where everything is perfect, just or equal.

INDEX

About the Author:
Jamia Wilson is the executive director and publisher of the Feminist Press. An activist and writer, Wilson has contributed to *New York Magazine*, the *New York Times*, *The Today Show*, CNN, BBC, *Teen Vogue*, *Elle*, Refinery 29, *Rookie*, and *The Guardian*. She is the author of *Young, Gifted, and Black* (Wide Eyed Editions), a co-author of *Road Map for Revolutionaries* (Ten Speed Press) and wrote the introduction and oral history to *Together We Rise: Behind the Scenes at the Protest Heard Around the World* (Dey Street Books).

About the Illustrator:
Andrea Pippins is an illustrator, designer, and author who has a passion for creating images that reflect what she wants to see in art, media, and pop culture. Her vision is to empower people of color with tools and inspiration to create and tell their own stories. She is the best-selling creator of the coloring book *I Love My Hair* and the interactive journal *Becoming Me*. Her clients include *O: The Oprah Magazine*, *Scoop Magazine*, *Family Circle*, *The Huffington Post*, *Bustle*, Free People, Lincoln Center, and the National Museum of African American History and Culture. Andrea is based in Stockholm, Sweden.

You might enjoy these books from the same author-illustrator team:

Step Into Your Power
978-1-78603-586-8

Young, Gifted, and Black
978-1-78603-158-7

A brightly illustrated guide that will teach you to harness your own power to achieve greatness. Make those big dreams a big reality. Learn from the lived experience of author Jamia Wilson and illustrator Andrea Pippins as they mentor you through growing up in the modern world, and teach you how to Step Into Your Power.

Meet 52 icons of color from past and present in this celebration of inspirational achievement— a collection of stories about changemakers to encourage, inspire and empower the next generation of changemakers. "...to be revisited again and again..."—New York Times

Inspiring | Educating | Creating | Entertaining

Brimming with creative inspiration, how-to projects, and useful information to enrich your everyday life, Quarto Knows is a favourite destination for those pursuing their interests and passions. Visit our site and dig deeper with our books into your area of interest: Quarto Creates, Quarto Cooks, Quarto Homes, Quarto Lives, Quarto Drives, Quarto Explores, Quarto Gifts, or Quarto Kids.

Big Ideas for Young Thinkers © 2020 Quarto Publishing plc.
Text © 2020 Jamia Wilson. Illustrations © 2020 Andrea Pippins.

First Published in 2020 by Wide Eyed Editions, an imprint of The Quarto Group.
400 First Avenue North, Suite 400, Minneapolis, MN 55401, USA.
T (612) 344-8100 F (612) 344-8692 **www.QuartoKnows.com**

The right of Andrea Pippins to be identified as the illustrator and Jamia Wilson to be identified as the author of this work has been asserted by them in accordance with the Copyright, Designs and Patents Act, 1988 (United Kingdom).

A catalog record for this book is available from the British Library.

ISBN 978-0-7112-4921-9

Published by Georgia Amson-Bradshaw
Edited and Commissioned by Katy Flint
Designed by Karissa Santos
Production by Dawn Cameron

Manufactured in Shenzhen, China PP122019
9 8 7 6 5 4 3 2 1

FSC
www.fsc.org
MIX
Paper from responsible sources
FSC® C001701